Burns and Blisters

Dr. Alvin Silverstein,

Virginia Silverstein, and

Laura Silverstein Nunn

My Health

Franklin Watts

A Division of Scholastic Inc.

New York • Toronto • London • Auckland • Sydney

Mexico City • New Delhi • Hong Kong

Danbury, Connecticut

Photographs © 2001: Corbis-Bettmann: 12, 22 (Lester V. Bergman), 20 (Reuters NewMedia Inc.); Fundamental Photos/Richard Megna: 6, 21; Peter Arnold Inc./Ed Reschke: 16; Photo Researchers, NY: 11 (John Bavosi/SPL), 23 top (Biophoto Associates), 7 (Biophoto Associates/SS), 13 (Scott Camazine), 17 top (Mike Devlin/SPL), 25 (Ray Ellis/SS), 29 (Gaillard/Jerrican), 23 bottom (Stevie Grand/SPL), 19 bottom (Dr. P. Marazzi/SPL), 31 (Oliver Meckes), 17 bottom (Garry Watson/SPL); PhotoEdit: 19 top (Peter D. Byron), 19 center, 37 (Michael Newman); Stock Boston/Bob Daemmrich: 26; Stone/Getty Images/Yorgos Nikas: 14; Superstock, Inc.: 9; The Image Works: 27 (Katharine Ciccarello), 18 (Pedrick), 38; Visuals Unlimited: 28 (Cabisco), 34 (Fred E. Hossler), 15 (David M. Phillips), 4 (D. Yeske).

Cartoons by Rick Stromoski

Library of Congress Cataloging-in-Publication Data

Silverstein, Alvin.
        Burns and Blisters / Alvin Silverstein, Virginia Silverstein, and Laura Silverstein Nunn.
            p.   cm.—(My Health)
        Includes bibliographical references and index.
        ISBN 0-531-11871-1 (lib. bdg.)   0-531-15561-7 (pbk.)
            1. Burns and scalds—Juvenile literature. 2. Blisters—Juvenile literature.
3. Skin—Wounds and injuries—Juvenile literature [1. Burns and scalds.
2. Wounds and injuries. 3. First aid.] I. Silverstein, Virginia B. II. Nunn, Laura Silverstein. III. Title. IV. Series.
RD96.4 .S545   2002
617.1′1—dc21   2001017571

Contents

That Burns!. 5

The Skin You Live In 7

What Happens When You Get Burned? 11

Kinds of Burns 18

Classifying Burns 22

Sunburn 25

Treating a Burn. 29

Protect Yourself!. 37

Glossary 40

Learning More 43

Index 46

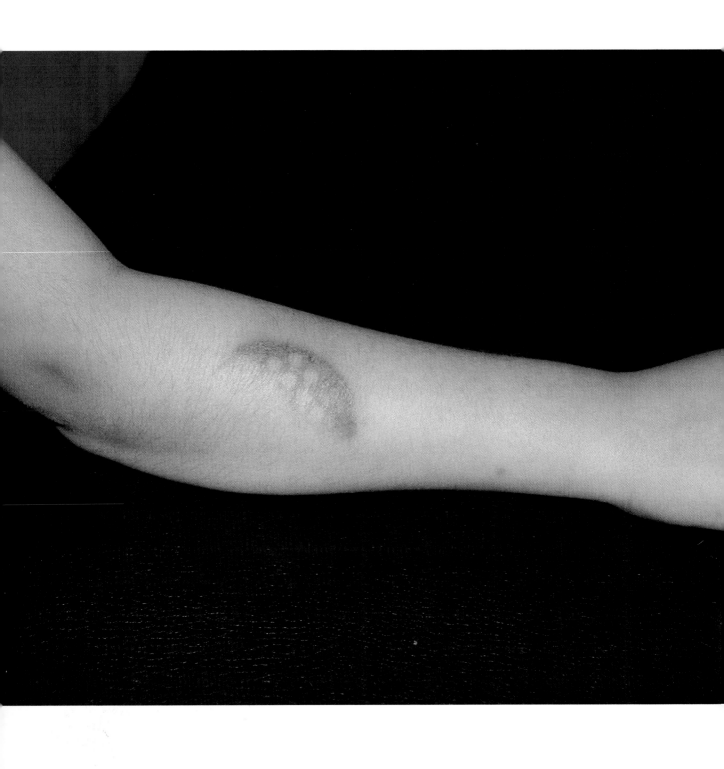

That Burns!

"Hot! Don't touch!" This is probably one of the first warnings your mom or dad taught you. If you were like many little kids, you may not have taken their word for it. You did your own hands-on experiment and found out the hard way—if you touch a hot stove, you will get burned, and burns can really hurt.

Anybody can get a burn. You can get burned in a number of different ways. Burns happen when your skin is damaged by fire, hot objects or liquids, certain chemicals, electricity, or the sun. Most burns are minor and can be treated at home. More serious burns may need immediate medical attention or even a stay in the hospital. Some burns are so serious that they may cause lasting health problems, disability, or even death.

Did You Know...

More than two million people in the United States get burned every year. Roughly seventy thousand people go to the hospital for severe burns. Those numbers don't include the many burns that are not reported because they are minor and are taken care of at home.

◀ **This is a minor burn caused by a hot object.**

Most burns can be prevented. By following some helpful tips, you can reduce your chances of getting burned. So read on to learn all about burns and what you can do to avoid them.

If you have to change a lightbulb, make sure you wait until the bulb is cool so you don't burn your hand.

The Skin You Live In

Your body is wrapped in a protective coating—your skin. The skin is the largest organ of the body. It makes up as much as 15 percent of your body weight. Like any other organ of the body, your skin does important jobs that help to keep you healthy.

Skin is soft and elastic, but it is strong. It can handle all kinds of wear and tear, and can even repair minor damage. It protects you, keeping dangerous chemicals and most germs from getting inside your body and harming you. At the same time, it keeps fluids inside and protects the body from drying out. Skin helps to keep your temperature constant, cooling you in hot weather and holding in warmth when it is cold outside. The skin is also a sense organ, letting you know about the

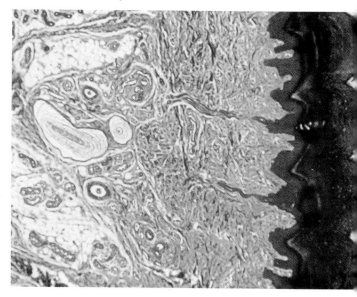

This is what the layers of your fingertip would look like if you magnified it more than 10,000 times.

7

world around you. Your skin is indeed remarkable, but it can get damaged in various ways.

The skin is made up of billions of tiny cells, each too small to see without a microscope. The cells in the skin that you see are actually dead. But new skin cells are constantly forming underneath them. They will move upward and eventually die too. Each skin cell lives an average of only 28 days.

The dead cells on the outside of your skin form a thick, tough protective layer. They are made mostly of a protein called *keratin*. You may not notice it, but some of the dead cells in this outer keratin layer are continually flaking off.

The keratin layer protects the living cells inside your body. It keeps out disease germs and also keeps body fluids from leaking out.

Just beneath the keratin layer there are two layers of living skin cells. The top layer is called the **epidermis**. The epidermis contains the cells that form the keratin layer when they die. The epidermis is very thin. It is only about as thick as a sheet of paper.

The epidermis lies on top of another layer of living skin cells called the **dermis**. The dermis makes up about 90 percent of the skin's thickness. It contains **glands** that give off sweat when you are hot, and other glands that produce oils when your skin is dry.

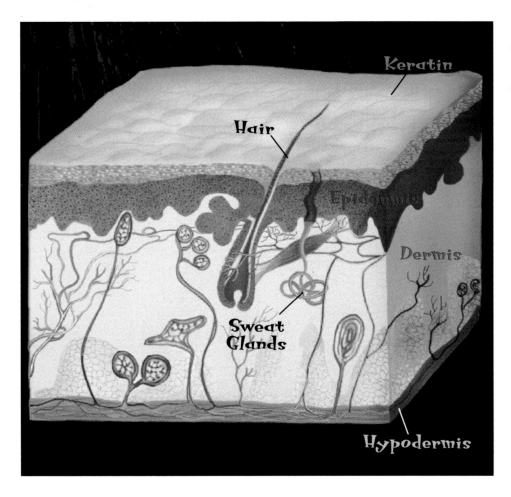

Here is a close-up look at the skin.

Keratin

Hair

Epidermis

Dermis

Sweat Glands

Hypodermis

Your hair grows out of **hair follicles** in the dermis. The dermis also contains nerve endings. Nerves in the dermis send messages to your brain about things you touch or feel. With a single touch, you can tell if an object is rough or smooth, hot or cold. If you touch something that is *too* hot or sharp enough to hurt you, nerve endings send pain messages to your brain that may make you say "Ouch!"

Skin cells need food and oxygen to live and grow. These important materials are carried in the blood by millions of tiny **blood vessels** that are found in the dermis. There are no blood vessels in the epidermis. That's why a shallow scratch doesn't bleed.

What Happens When You Get Burned?

When you burn your skin on a hot stove, skin cells are destroyed by the heat. The damaged skin cells send out chemicals that act as alarm signals. They tell the body that something is wrong. These chemicals also trigger the surrounding nerves, causing you to feel pain.

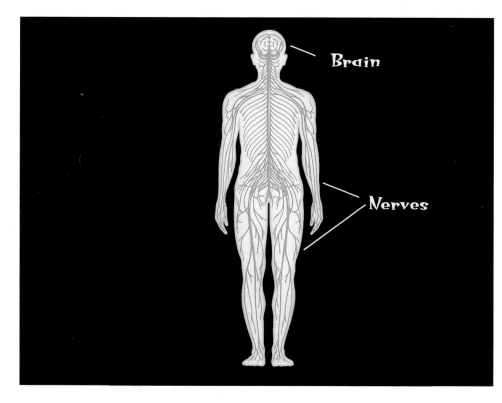

Your brain controls many parts of your body by sending and receiving messages. Nerves carry those messages to and from the brain.

Mixed Signals

Your body's pain signals can get mixed up sometimes. An ice cube feels "burning hot" because your nerves are triggered by extreme temperatures, which include both hot and cold.

Plasma is the clear fluid in your blood.

Some of these chemicals cause **plasma**—the clear fluid in blood—to leak out of nearby blood vessels into body tissues, making them swollen. The tissues also become hot and red. This process is called **inflammation**.

As the heat kills skin cells, layers of the epidermis and possibly the dermis become separated. Plasma then seeps into the gap and fills it up, causing a bubblelike **blister** to form.

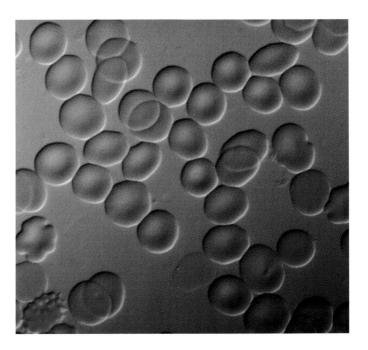

Don't Burst a Blister

When you get a cut or scrape, the blood vessels in the skin may be broken, causing you to bleed. Eventually, a jellylike substance called a **clot** forms and plugs up the hole. When the blood dries, the blood clot forms a hard **scab** over the wound. Scabs help to protect your skin from further damage while it heals. Burns, on the other hand, do not bleed. But a blister protects the damaged tissues underneath just as a scab protects a cut.

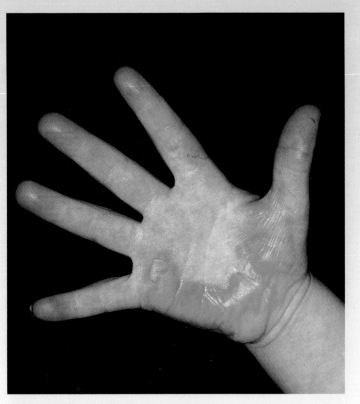

The skin creates a blister to protect the burned skin as it heals.

A blister looks like a little bubble, but you need to be careful not to burst it. If a blister is opened, **bacteria** can get inside and cause an **infection**. Also, the exposed tissues might get damaged even more, which may cause bleeding and then scabbing. Eventually, the burned tissue underneath the blister heals. The plasma seeps back into the tissues, and the blister gets smaller. Finally, the dead part peels off when it is no longer needed for protection.

Meanwhile, the damaged blood vessels also release chemicals that send signals. They call in jellylike **white blood cells** that can move through blood and tissues.

White blood cells can move most easily through inflamed, fluid-filled tissues. They squeeze out of tiny holes in walls of the blood vessels and move through the fluid in the gaps between the cells. The white blood cells act like a clean-up squad. When they come into contact with the damaged tissue, they eat up dead cells and bits of dirt in the wound.

What happens next depends on how much damage there is. The body's major job is healing: repairing the damage so that the skin is whole again. In minor burns—those that do not go below the epidermis—the healing process is fairly simple. Skin cells in the tissues around the burn start to multiply. Each cell divides in half to form two smaller skin cells. These new skin cells grow quickly and move into the wound area. There they continue to grow and multiply until the gap is filled in with new skin.

This is what your white and red blood cells would look like if they were magnified over 10,000 times.

Burns can get infected easily because when the protective outer layers of skin are gone, your body tissues are exposed, making it easier for germs to get inside. If an infection develops, the damaged cells call in the white blood cells, which quickly arrive to attack the foreign invaders. They gobble up germs and damaged cells. But germs produce poisons, and after a white blood cell has eaten a lot of them, it dies. **Pus**, that yucky white stuff that builds up when you have an infection, is made up mainly of the bodies of dead white cell defenders, along with the germs they have killed.

For severe burns—those that are very large or very deep—the healing process is a bit more complicated. As the cells multiply and move up into the wound, some of these are new skin cells and some are **fibroblasts**. Fibroblasts are cells that form tough threads of protein that build a framework over the damaged area. They also pull the edges of the wound together so that there is a smaller gap to fill. Both skin

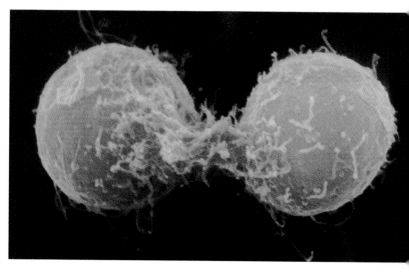

These two cells are almost finished dividing.

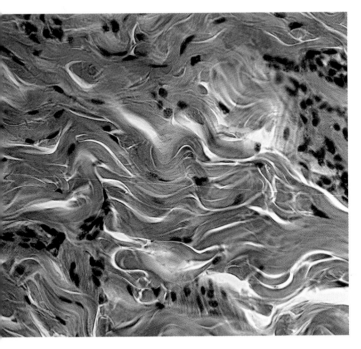

This is what fibroblasts look like magnified over 10,000 times.

cells and fibroblasts multiply, gradually filling in the gap. A protein called **collagen**, is made by the fibroblasts and acts as a glue and a support.

The new skin that forms to close the gap contains a lot of collagen fibers in addition to the epidermis and dermis cells. The areas of collagen form a scar, which does not look quite like normal skin. It does not have the chemicals that give skin its usual color, and no hair grows out of the scarred area. But the collagen fibers make scar tissue much stronger than normal skin. The size of a burn scar depends on how much tissue was damaged. More collagen is needed to cover a larger gap, and healing, therefore, leaves a bigger scar.

How long a burn takes to heal depends on how serious the skin damage. Mild burns heal rather quickly, in about one to two weeks, with little or no scarring. More severe burns, however, can take much longer to repair (possibly months or even years) and there is often a lot of scarring.

Scar tissue does the job of closing up a wound and covering the burn tissue with a strong, protective layer. But the collagen fibers are so strong that they may pull the surounding tissues together too tightly. Scar tissue that forms on a burned hand, for example, may make it hard to move the fingers.

Doctors may be able to prevent scars from developing or repair scar tissue with *skin grafts*. These are thin layers of skin taken from another part of the body to cover a wound. Artificial tissue grown in a laboratory, may also be used for skin grafts. The living skin cells in the graft multiply and cover the damaged area with new skin. Then there is no scar. But for people with severe burns, getting rid of scars may not be possible.

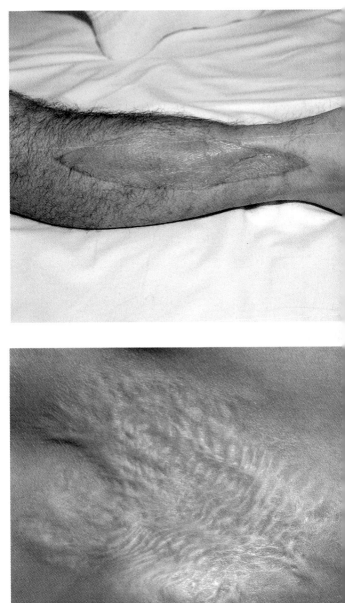

Doctors can use a skin graft to repair a severe burn, preventing the formation of scars.

Kinds of Burns

Most burns occur at home. There are a number of different things that can burn you. The most common kind of burn is caused by dry heat. You can get this kind of burn by coming into contact with fire, stoves, ovens, irons, heaters, or even a lightbulb.

Whenever you take something out of the oven, be sure to use pot holders.

If you hop into a shower or bath and the water is too hot, you can **scald** your skin. Scalds are burns that are caused by hot liquids or steam (water in gas form). You can scald the inside of your mouth or throat by drinking a steaming cup of hot chocolate. Or you can scald your hand by touching the steam that comes out of a pot of boiling water.

Certain chemicals can also produce burns. For instance, chlorine bleach or very strong cleaning products can burn your skin. Gasoline can burn you too.

Electricity can be very dangerous. If you touch a frayed electric cord, you will receive a shock that feels like a painful punch. You may also get burned. Even if you don't see any damage to your skin, the electric shock may have caused serious burns inside your body. If this happens, go see a doctor.

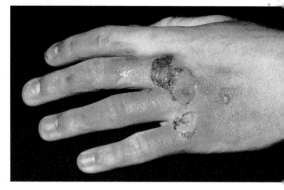

A shower that is too hot can scald your skin (above). Hot liquids can scald your tongue (center). This scald was caused by hot liquid or steam (right).

Activity 1:
What's Rug Burn?

Have you ever tripped while running indoors and gone sliding along the carpet? If you were wearing shorts, you probably wound up with red, hot, painful knees. They weren't exactly like the  scraped knees you get when you fall outdoors. The skin wasn't broken and they weren't bleeding. You actually had a kind of burn. Baseball players sometimes get this kind of injury too. Even though their long pants protect them from scrapes, sliding into a base on a close play can give them a "raspberry"—a painful red patch on the outside of the thigh.

How can you get a burn without touching anything hot? Actually, there was heat involved and you yourself helped to create it. When you slid, your knees rubbed against the carpet. And when two solids rub against each other, the **friction** between them generates heat.

To find out for yourself just how much heat friction can produce, you'll need an indoor-outdoor thermometer—the kind that has a small metal probe attached to a wire. First tape the probe to the palm of your hand with a small piece of sticky tape and leave it in place for a minute (or until the temperature on the thermometer stays steady). Write down that temperature and then remove the probe and rub the palms of your hands against each other as hard and fast as you can. You'll feel the heat building up between them. Now slip the thermometer probe between your palms and hold them tightly together until you get a steady temperature reading. How many degrees did the friction raise the temperature of your palms?

Your palms are smooth, so the friction between them didn't make enough heat to burn you. But rubbing against the rough surface of a carpet can give you a mild "rug burn."

Classifying Burns

Doctors separate burns into three categories, depending on how serious they are.

A minor burn is called a **first-degree burn**. The skin is swollen, reddened, and painful. Only the outer layer (the epidermis) is damaged. Briefly touching a hot object, such as a stove or iron, is a common cause of first-degree burns.

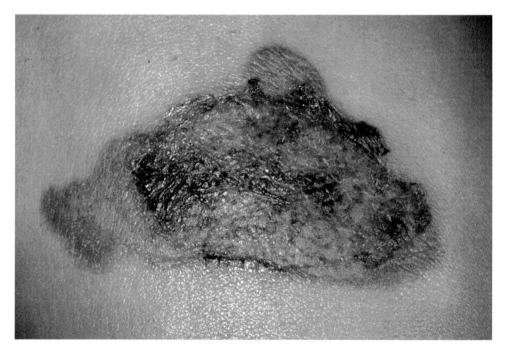

This is a first degree burn.

A **second-degree burn** is a more serious burn that affects both the outer skin layer and the one underneath it (the epidermis and the dermis). Fluid-filled blisters usually develop in second-degree burns.

The most serious type of burn is a **third-degree burn**. In this case, all the skin layers are destroyed, as are some of the tissues underneath. The skin may look white, very red, or even blackened. Plasma leaks out of the tissues, but blisters do not form because the upper layers of skin are gone. You would think that this kind of burn is extremely painful. Actually, many patients with third-degree burns don't feel any pain at all because the nerve endings in their skin have been destroyed. A person with a third-degree burn may need a lot of skin grafting. As the wounds heal, major scars form.

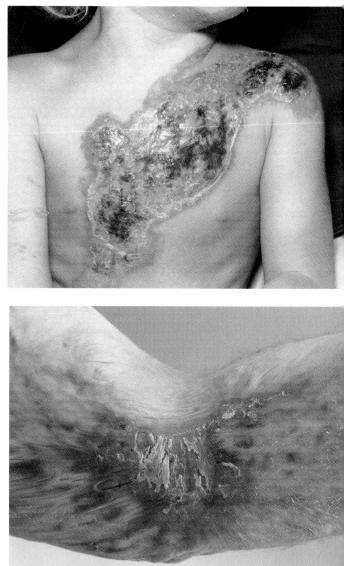

The top photo is a second-degree burn. The bottom photo is a third-degree burn.

Fire is a common cause of third-degree burns. People who survive fires may be left with burns that cover much of their bodies. When this happens, serious or even life-threatening complications may develop.

Going into Shock

Severe burns can be very dangerous. The body loses a lot of fluids when it is burned. These fluids are needed to keep the heart and kidneys working properly and the body cells supplied with the oxygen and nutrients they need to function. Lack of these fluids can put a person into **shock**. Some early signs of shock may include a pale face; cold, sweaty hands and feet; shallow, fast breathing; weak pulse rate; and confusion. Later, the person may be very restless and thirsty, may have trouble breathing, and may possibly lose consciousness. Health workers need to look for signs of shock when they are treating third-degree burn victims.

SHOCK
PaLe
SWEATS
HYPERVENTILATE
WEAK PuLse

Sunburn

A day at the beach is a lot of fun on a hot summer day. But if you're not careful, a day of fun in the sun can lead to a very uncomfortable night. Sunburn is one of the most common kinds of burns. The sun sends out harmful **ultraviolet rays** (UV rays) that can make your skin red and painful when you stay out in it for too long. Sunburn is a warning that UV rays have hurt your skin. Even though the sunburn eventually goes away, the injury to the skin remains. Some studies show that kids who get sunburned have a higher risk of getting skin cancer as adults.

This girl has sunburn, one of the most common kinds of burns.

Are Tans Healthy?

Some people think that a tan makes you look healthy. But the truth is that when you get a tan, you are actually damaging your skin. Even being exposed to artificial sunlight from a tanning salon can damage your skin. So basically, there is no such thing as a "safe tan."

Most sunburns are first-degree burns and they are often very painful. When sunburn covers much of your body, it may be too painful to do your everyday activities, especially sleeping.

You can avoid getting sunburned by putting on sunscreen or sunblock. Sunscreen lotion soaks up some of the sun's UV rays so they never get a chance to hurt your skin. Sunblock is even better. It keeps *all* of the UV rays from reaching your skin. When you put on sunscreen or sunblock, you are putting on an invisible

Make sure you use sunscreen or sunblock whenever you are in the sun.

suit of armor. The best sunscreens and sunblocks have a Sun Protection Factor (SPF) of 15 or higher. If you sweat a lot or go swimming, though, the water will wash away your protection. So be sure to reapply these lotions frequently.

Be sure to reapply sunscreen every few hours, more often if you are in the water.

Does Everybody Get Sunburned?

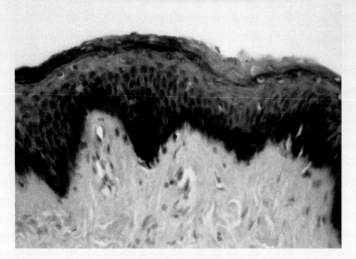

This is what melanin looks like when magnified more than 10,000 times.

Anyone can get sunburned—no matter what color their skin. However, people with light-colored skin burn more easily and more severely than those with dark-colored skin. Human skin contains tiny black grains called **melanin** that protect us from the sun's harmful rays. Dark skin contains more melanin than light skin, so it can handle more sun. But the protection isn't complete, so dark-skinned people need to use sunscreen or sunblock too.

The ancestors of people with dark skin came from Africa, Central America, and other places where the sun is very bright and hot. The ancestors of people with very light skin came from Norway, Sweden, and other places where the sun is not as strong.

Treating a Burn

Most burns are mild and can be treated at home. For a first-degree burn, the first thing to do is to remove any clothing close to the skin unless it is stuck to the burn. Then quickly run cool water over the burn for eight to fifteen minutes. This will help reduce the pain and swelling. The burn should then be covered with a dry, clean dressing (made of non-stick gauze) to protect it from germs. If the burn wound starts to ooze, see a doctor.

If you burn your hand, make sure you put it under cold water right away.

Don't Butter a Burn

People used to think that applying butter to burns helped heal them. But this does not really help. In fact, it may make the injury worse. Butter holds in heat and may damage the skin. So don't put butter or any kind of greasy ointment on a burn.

A cool bath can help to ease the pain of sunburn. Creams and lotions that are not greasy can also make you more comfortable and help healing. Pain medications like acetaminophen or ibuprofen may be helpful, too. Ibuprofen not only eases pain, but also reduces swelling and inflammation.

For more serious burns—when blisters develop or the skin is broken, you may need to see a doctor. The wound must be cleaned thoroughly and wrapped in clean dressings to avoid infection. Sometimes **tetanus** bacteria may get inside a burn and cause serious trouble.

Tetanus bacteria don't cause too much trouble in shallow wounds, but they multiply quickly in deep cuts or severe burns. If these bacteria spread into your bloodstream, they can cause a condition called lockjaw. Your muscles get so stiff that you can't move. You can't even open your mouth to eat or talk. Tetanus bacteria can even cause death. Babies are given shots to protect them against tetanus, but the protection doesn't last forever. You should get a booster shot every 10 years to stay protected.

People with severe burns—those that cover more than 10 percent of the body—should go to the hospital. A doctor must remove the damaged, often blackened skin quickly so that healthy skin can grow. A skin graft is usually needed to cover the burned area. This is especially true for burns that cover the face, feet, and hands, where severe scarring could limit movement.

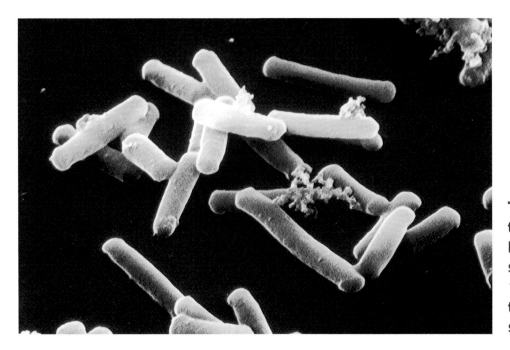

These are tetanus bacteria shown 10,000 times their real size.

Activity 2:
Make a Burn Chart

A poster can help you identify first-, second-, and third-degree burns and remember what to do to treat them. You'll need a sheet of white posterboard, sheets of black and red construction paper, a sandwich-size plastic bag, scissors, sticky tape, and glue.

Leave a 3-inch space at the top of the posterboard for the title "Kinds of Burns." Draw three 2-inch circles evenly spaced in a row. Carefully cut along the circles you drew so you have three 2-inch round holes in the poster-board. Lay this sheet on top of the red construction paper and trace inside the third circle, marking it on the red paper. Cut out that circle carefully. Don't cut any holes in the black construction paper. Glue or tape the three sheets together, with the white posterboard on top, the red construction paper in the middle, and the black paper on the bottom. You will see red showing through the first two holes in the posterboard and black through the third. Now take the plastic bag, blow into it, and then fold over the edge, trapping a bubble of air inside. Tape down the fold so you won't lose the air, then fold in the corners and edges so that the bubble is about the right size to fit over the middle hole in the poster. Glue or tape it in place. Neatly print labels under each circle.

First-degree burn	Second-degree burn	Third-degree burn
Skin red and hot	Redness, blisters, pain	Skin appears white or black
What to do	**What to do**	**What to do**
Run cold water over the burn or apply a cold compress. Cover with a clean bandage.	Clean carefully and apply a clean bandage. Don't burst the blister! See a doctor if the burn is large or gets infected	Cover the burn with a clean bandage and see a doctor right away. While recovering, drink plenty of juice and soup and eat foods that contain protein and vitamins.

A person with severe burns needs to drink a lot of fluids to replace the large amount of fluids that were lost. Remember that when you get burned, you lose plasma. The larger the burned area, the more plasma that is lost. This can be very dangerous because plasma contains proteins, salts, and other important materials that body cells need to live. Clear soups and fruit juices help to replace the lost fluids and other materials. If the burns are very serious, the person may need a **transfusion**. Blood or plasma is dripped into the person's body through a tube with a hollow needle inserted into a blood vessel.

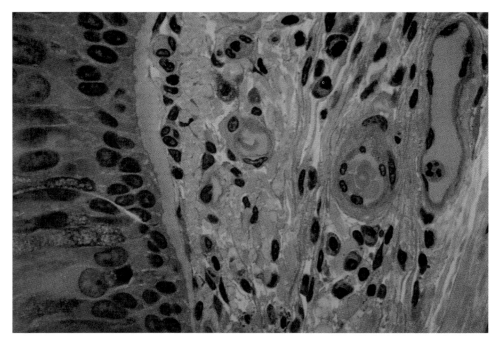

This is plasma from the blood magnified 10,000 times its real size.

Burn victims also need extra protein and extra **calories** in their diets to help fight off infection and grow new tissue. Calories are important because they give the body the energy it needs to heal.

What you eat is also very important in the healing process. Some vitamins can help burns heal faster. Vitamin A helps to keep your skin strong. Vitamin C helps to keep your body's defenses against infection strong and speed the healing process. Vitamin C is also needed for making collagen, the glue that holds tissues together. Some studies have found that people who took vitamin C after a burn lost a lot less fluid than those who did not take vitamin C. Vitamin E helps to heal burns too. Vitamin E also helps to make collagen to help wounds heal. Vitamin E comes in liquid capsules and can be put directly on a burn, which can help to reduce scarring or even prevent scars from developing. A mineral called selenium helps vitamin E to work.

Did You Know...

The average child needs about 2,300 calories every day. A child with burn injuries needs 3,000 or more calories a day.

Foods That Help You Heal

Vitamin A	Vitamin C	Vitamin E	Selenium
Broccoli	Cantaloupe	Margarine	Beef
Carrots	Grapefruit	Olives	Chicken
Eggs	Green peppers	Vegetable oil	Eggs
Liver	Lemons	Wheat germ	Fish
Milk	Limes	Whole grains	Shellfish
Sweet potatoes	Oranges		Wheat germ
Yellow squash	Tomatoes		Whole grains
Zucchini			

Protect Yourself!

Burns can make you feel miserable. Even a minor burn can really hurt. A severe burn could change your life forever, or even kill you. So what can you do to protect yourself and avoid getting burned in the first place?

You can stay safe by following some important safety rules. Be careful around hot objects, including stoves, irons, curling irons, and radiators. You can't always tell when they're hot just by looking at them. If you help out with cooking, you should ask an adult to help you use the stove or oven. And if you do ever handle anything hot, always wear protective, fireproof oven mitts. Don't fool around with electrical outlets and never put anything in

Do you protect yourself when you are cooking or helping someone cook?

them, especially your fingers. Don't play with electrical appliances and never use them near water. Getting water on a working electric hair dryer, radio, or lamp might cause a short circuit. That could lead to a fire or give you a bad electric shock.

Do you practice fire safety? Never play with matches or cigarette lighters. Gasoline, chemical cleaning fluids, and starter fluids for outdoor grills can flare up

How often are the batteries in the smoke detectors in your home changed?

suddenly if there is an open flame or spark nearby. They should be used only by adults. Firecrackers are another big fire hazard that can explode and cause serious injuries. They are not toys and should be handled only by professionals.

Make sure there are smoke detectors throughout your house, especially near the bedrooms. Smoke alarms should be checked often. A good way to stay safe is to change the batteries every time you turn your clocks forward in the spring and back in the fall.

Would you know what to do in a fire? You should practice fire drills with your parents so you know what to do in case there's a fire and find the safest ways to get out of your house. If your clothes catch on fire, do you know what to do? Remember to STOP, DROP, and ROLL. This will put out the fire and save you from further harm. It may even save your life.

There are also things you can do to help your body heal more quickly if you do get burned. Staying fit will help keep you ready to meet any challenge—even the huge job of rebuilding damaged tissues. That means getting enough sleep, getting regular exercise, and eating the right foods, including plenty of fruits and vegetables. All these things have a very important effect on how you feel and how you heal.

Glossary

bacteria—germs; single-celled organisms too small to see without a microscope. Some bacteria cause diseases when they get into the body.

blister—a bubble like lump on the skin that contains a watery liquid called plasma

blood vessel—a tube that carries blood through the body

calorie—the unit of measurement of the amount of energy stored in foods

clot—a jellylike solid formed by blood to close up a wound. When exposed to air, it gets dry and hard.

collagen—a protein that acts as a glue and support for skin and other tissues

dermis—the inner layer of living skin cells located beneath the epidermis. This layer also contains nerves and blood vessels.

epidermis—the top layer of living skin cells

fibroblasts—fiber-forming cells that make the framework for skin and connective tissues

first-degree burn—a mild burn; a painful reddening and swelling of the epidermis

friction—rubbing of one surface against another

glands—organs in the dermis that give off sweat and oil

hair follicle—the tubelike structure in the skin from which a hair grows

infection—invasion of the body by germs that multiply and damage tissues

inflammation—redness, heat, and swelling that develop when tissues are damaged

keratin—a protein found in skin, hair, and nails

melanin—dark pigment in the skin

plasma—the clear fluid in blood

pus—a whitish substance containing the bodies of dead white blood cells and bacteria

scab—the dried remains of a blood clot that closed up a wound. It acts as a protective cover under which a wound heals.

scald—a burn caused by a hot liquid or steam

scar—tough, strong tissue containing collagen fibers that connects the cut edges of a wound

second-degree burn—damage to both the epidermis and dermis that usually involves blistering

shock—a condition in which a person's organs are not receiving enough oxygen and nutrients to function normally as a result of serious wounds, including burns

skin graft—moving a thin layer of healthy skin from another part of the body to cover a wound so that a scar will not form

tetanus—a dangerous disease caused by bacteria that can grow only where there is no air, such as in deep wounds or severe burns

third-degree burn—the destruction of the epidermis and dermis extending into deeper tissues. Nerve endings may also be destroyed

transfusion—transferring blood or plasma into the blood vessel of a person

ultraviolet rays—powerful sun rays that can damage a person's skin

white blood cells—jellylike blood cells that can move through tissues and are an important part of the body's defenses. Some white blood cells eat germs and clean up bits of damaged cells and dirt.

Learning More

Books

American Medical Association. *Handbook of First Aid and Emergency Care.* New York: Random House, 2000.

Carter, Albert Howard and Jane A. Pietro. *Rising from the Flames: The Experience of the Severely Burned*, Philadelphia. University of Pennsylvania Press, 1998. [Advanced Reading Level]

Cole, Joanna. *Cuts, Breaks, Bruises, and Burns*, New York. HarperCollins Publishers, 1985.

Lucile Salter Packard Children's Hospital at Stanford. *Family First Aid.* Palo Alto: Klutz, 1997.

Munster, Andrew M. *Severe Burns: A Family Guide to Medical and Emotional Recovery.* Baltimore: Johns Hopkins University Press, 1993. [Advanced Reading Level]

Organizations and Internet Sites

Alisa Ann Ruch Burn Foundation
http://www.aarbf.org/
This organization provides prevention materials (many free) including brochures, videos, stickers, magnets, and posters.

Burn Facts
http://www.burnfree.com/burnfact.htm
This site offers facts and statistics about burn-related injuries.

Burns
http://kidshealth.org/parent/firstaid_safe/emergencies/burns.html
This KidsHealth.org site, provided by the Nemours Foundation, includes basic information about burns and first-aid treatment.

Fire Prevention Cooking Advice
http://firesafety.buffnet.net/cook.htm

Georgia Firefighters Burn Foundation Kids Play
http://www.gfbf.org/kidsplay.shtml
Fun safety and fire prevention activities including a coloring book and poster to print out.

How to Be Safe When You're in the Sun
http://kidshealth.org/parent/firstaid_safe/outdoor/sun_safety_prt.htm
This KidsHealth.org site includes information about sunburn and how to protect yourself from the sun's dangerous rays.

Koola's Arcade
http://www.kidsafetyhouse.com/kids/kids.htm
Print-out activities to color and play from Berks County Kid's Safety House.

National Burn Information Exchange (NBIE)
National Institute for Burn Medicine
9600 East Ann Street
Ann Arbor, MI 48104
(313) 769-9000

Sparky the Fire Dog
http://www.sparky.org/
Fun activities from the official "spokesdog" of the National Fire
Protection Agency (NFPA).

Sun Safety
http://kidshealth.org/parent/firstaid_safe/outdoor/sun_safety_prt.htm
This KidsHealth.org site includes information about the dangers of sun exposure and how to protect yourself from the sun's dangerous rays.

The Burn Institute
3702 Ruffin Road, Suite 101
San Diego, CA 92123-1842
(858) 541-2277

Index

Page numbers in *italics* indicate illustrations.

Acetaminophen, 30
Artificial tissue, 17

Bacteria, 13, 30-31, *31*, 40
Bleeding, 10, 13, 20
Blister, 12-13, *13*, 30, 33, 40
Blood, 10, 12, *12*, 13, 14, 30,
    34, *34*
Blood vessel, 10, 12, 13, 14,
    34, 40
Body fluids, 7, 8, 24
Body temperature, 7, 9
Booster shot, 31
Brain, 10, *11*
Burn chart, 32-33
Burns, 11, 12
    categories, 22, *22*, 23, *23*
    causes, 5, 6, *6*, 11, 18, 19,
       19, 25
    minor, 5, *5*, 14, 16, 22, 29, 37
    safety, 18, 37, *37*, 38, *38*,39
    severe, 5, 15-17, 23, *23*, 24,
       30, 31, 34, 37
    treatment, 29, *29*, 30, 32
Calorie, 35, 40
Chemical burn, 19

Clot, 13, 40
Collagen, 16, 17, 35, 40

Dermis, 9, *9*, 10, 12, 16, 23, 40
Dry heat burn, 18

Electric shock, 19, 37, 38
Epidermis, 8-10, 12, 14, 16, 22,
    23, 40

Fibroblasts, 15, 16, *16*, 40
Fire, 24, 38, 39
Firecracker, 39
Fire drill, 39
First-degree burn, 22, *22*, 26,
    29, 32-33, 41
Fitness, 39
Foods, 36, 39
Friction, 20, 21, 41

Germs, 7, 8, 15, 29
Glands, 9, 41

Hair follicle, *9*, 10, 41
Healing, 14, 36
    blister, 13, *13*

burn, 15-17, 35, 36, 39
Hypodermis, *9*

Ibuprofen, 30
Infection, 13, 15, 30, 33, 35, 41
Inflammation, 12, 41

Keratin, 8, 9, 41

Lockjaw, 30

Melanin, 28, *28*, 41

Nerves, 10, 11, *11*, 12, 23

Pain, 10-12, 23, 25-26, 29, 30, 33
Plasma, 12-13, 23, 34, *34*, 41
Proteins, 8, 15, 16, 33, 34, 35
Pus, 15, 41

Raspberry, 20
Red blood cells, *14*
Rug burn, 20-21

Scab, 13, 41
Scald, 19, *19*, 41
Scar, 16-17, *17*, 23, 31, 35, 42
Second-degree burn, 23, *23*, 32-33, 42
Selenium, 35, 36
Sense organ, 7

Shock, 19, 24, 37, 38, 42
Skin, 7, *13*, 13-16, *17*, 20
    components of, 7-9, *9*, 28
    injury to, 25-26
Skin cancer, 25
Skin cells, 8, 10, 11, 12
    healing, 14-15, *15*, 16, 17
Skin graft, 17, *17*, 23, 31, 42
Smoke detector, *38*, 39
Steam, 19, *19*
Sunblock, 26, *26*, 27, 28
Sunburn, 25, *25*, 26, 28, 30
Sun Protection Factor, 27
Sunscreen, 26, *26*, 27, *27*, 28
Sweat, 9, 24, 27
Sweat gland, 9, *9*

Tan, 26
Tetanus, 30, 31, *31*, 42
Third-degree burns, 23, *23*, 24, 32-33, 42
Transfusion, 34, 42

Ultraviolet rays, 25, 26, 42

Vitamin, 33, 35, 36
Vitamin A, 35, 36
Vitamin C, 35, 36
Vitamin E, 35, 36

White blood cells, 14, *14*, 15, 42

About the Authors

Dr. Alvin Silverstein is a Professor of Biology at the College of Staten Island of the City University of New York. **Virginia B. Silverstein** is a translator of Russian scientific literature. The Silversteins first worked together on a research project at the University of Pennsylvania. Since then, they have produced 6 children and more than 170 published books for young people.

Laura Silverstein Nunn, a graduate of Kean College, has been helping with her parents' books since her high-school days. She is the coauthor of more than fifty books on diseases and health, science concepts, endangered species, and pets. Laura lives with her husband Matt and their young son Cory in a rural New Jersey town not far from her childhood home.